SAFE HARBOR

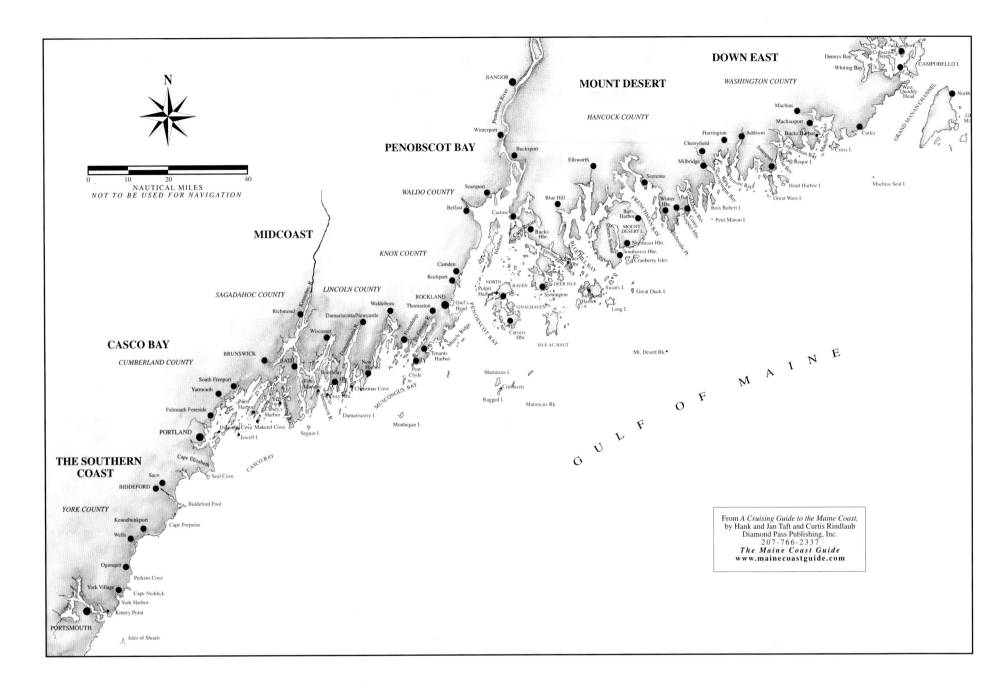

N

NAUTICAL MILES
0   10   20   40
NOT TO BE USED FOR NAVIGATION

DOWN EAST

Dennys Bay
Cobscook Bayer
Eastport
CAMPOBELLO I.
Whiting Bay
Lubec
West Quoddy Head
North

MOUNT DESERT

WASHINGTON COUNTY

BANGOR

Machias
Machiasport

HANCOCK COUNTY

Winterport

Harrington   Addison   Bucks Harbor
Cherryfield   Englishman Bay   Cross I.
Cutler

Bucksport

Milbridge   Jonesport   Roque I.

PENOBSCOT BAY

Ellsworth

Sorrento

Pleasant Bay
Head Harbor I.
Great Wass I.
Machias Seal I.

Searsport

WALDO COUNTY

Blue Hill

Winter Hbr.

Bois Bubert I.
Petit Manan I.

Belfast

Castine

FRENCHMAN BAY
Prospect Hbr.
Corea Hbr.
Schoodic Pt.

MIDCOAST

Cape Rosier
Bucks Hbr.

Bar Harbor

MOUNT DESERT I.
Northeast Hbr.
Southwest Hbr.
Cranberry Isles

KNOX COUNTY

Islesboro

Eggemoggin Reach
BLUE HILL BAY
Stonington Swan's I.
Great Duck I.

Camden
Rockport

NORTH HAVEN
Pulpit Harbor

DEER ISLE
Stonington
Burntcoat Harbor
Long I.

CASCO BAY

SAGADAHOC COUNTY

LINCOLN COUNTY

ROCKLAND
Thomaston

Owl's Head

VINALHAVEN

CUMBERLAND COUNTY

Richmond
Waldoboro

Damariscotta/Newcastle

Friendship
St. George R.

Music Ridge

Carvers Hbr.

ISLE AU HAUT

Mt. Desert Rk.

BRUNSWICK
Wiscasset

BATH

New Harbor

Tenants Harbor

GULF OF MAINE

South Freeport
Yarmouth

Boothbay
Boothbay Hbr.

Port Clyde

Matinicus I.

Falmouth Foreside

Five Islands

Christmas Cove

Criehaven

Potts Harbor
Cundy's Harbor
Cozy Hbr.

Ragged I.
Matinicus Rk.

PORTLAND

Diamond Cove Makerel Cove

Damariscove I.

Monhegan I.

Jewell I.

Seguin I.

Cape Elizabeth

THE SOUTHERN COAST

Saco

Seal Cove

CASCO BAY

BIDDEFORD

YORK COUNTY

Biddeford Pool

Kennebunkport

Cape Porpoise

Wells

Ogunquit   Perkins Cove

York Village
Cape Neddick
York Harbor

Kittery Point

PORTSMOUTH

Isles of Shoals

From *A Cruising Guide to the Maine Coast*,
by Hank and Jan Taft and Curtis Rindlaub
Diamond Pass Publishing, Inc.
207-766-2337
The Maine Coast Guide
www.mainecoastguide.com

SAFE HARBOR

Exploring Maine's Protected Bays, Coves, and Anchorages

William Hubbell
Captions by Jean Hubbell

 Down East Books, Camden, Maine

To our editor, Chris Cornell,
with our deepest thanks for his vision,
his patience, and his magic with words.

Interior and jacket design by Lindy Gifford
Printed in China

5   4   3   2   1

ISBN 0-89272-562-1
Library of Congress Control Number: 2003104360

Cover photograph:
Smack in the middle of Penobscot Bay, just above North Haven,
sits the Barred Island mini-archipelago, forming one of the most
beautiful, unspoiled anchorages on Maine's coast.

Title page photograph:
At the Perry Creek anchorage on the northern tip of Vinalhaven,
a venerable 1930s-era power yacht swings at anchor in the late
afternoon glow.

Back cover photographs:
Maine harbors come in all shapes and sizes. Some of them, like
Perkins Cove (top) in Ogunquit and Bar Harbor (bottom) on
Mount Desert Island are regular stops for both yachtsmen and
tourists. Others, like Mackerel Cove (center) on Bailey Island,
offer shelter off the beaten track.

Down East Books
P.O. Box 679
Camden, ME 04843
www.downeastbooks.com

Acknowledgments

A harbor, even if it is a little harbor, is a good thing, since adventures come into it as well as go out, and the life in it grows strong, because it takes something from the world and has something to give in return.

—Sarah Orne Jewett, from *River Driftwood (1881)*

Harbors (and anchorages) are indeed good things. The coast of Maine is blessed with more than its share of places where one can find both great beauty and protected water. That they would make a good subject for a picture book is the brainchild of our creative and gently discerning editor, Chris Cornell, who launched the idea and then let us sail with it. The fact that we didn't own a boat seemed not to faze him in the least.

To photograph a book on Maine's harbors and gunkholes without a hull to convey us was at first a daunting task. However, contacts rapidly developed. Soon we had a squadron of helpers, then a fleet, and in time an armada of support. In these acknowledgments, there is room to mention only a few of the many who contributed to this effort.

The admiral of this navy would have to be Dick Kurtz. With his boat *Blue Dolphin*, captured on the dust jacket, Dick took me around the central part of Maine's coast, visiting forty harbors and anchorages in seven days, including some twenty offshore islands. My thanks also to Down East Books publisher Neale Sweet for an overnight sail to anchorages along Penobscot Bay's Muscle Ridge Channel, and to Captain Ray Williamson of the windjammer *Mercantile*.

Those who contributed their time and talents in front of the camera deserve our thanks, as well. First I must mention the six generous people who each introduce their section of Maine's coast—Bill Kingston, Lisa Plummer, Peter Kass, Neal Parker, Ted Hoskins, and Colby Young. Then there were Gus Pratt of the Cosy Harbor Store on Southport Island; boat transporter Mike Devine and Harbormaster Steve Pixley, both of Camden; and John McCollett, the harbormaster in Kittery.

There were also many helpers behind the scenes: Thanks go to graphic designer Lindy Gifford for giving this work a most pleasing balance between pictures and text and who has now laid out both our volumes for Down East Books; to Curtis Rindlaub, editor of the *Cruising Guide to the Maine Coast* for the use of his excellent map; to Roger Taylor for an extensive list of little-known harbors and anchorages; to Rear Admiral Richard Rybacki, USCG, ret. , and Bill Crowe, editor of *The Fishermen's Voice* for information and advice; to Heidi Lackey and Amanda Lackey for generating countless picture labels; and to Fred Field and his young assistant, Robert, for the fine photograph of me and my wife, Jeannie, the shot that appears on the jacket flap.

Last, kudos go to Jeannie for having been such a supportive and hard-working cocaptain of this pictorial cruise in and out of the nooks and crannies of Maine's coast. She assumed the tedious job of labeling and filing literally thousands of slides. Jeannie also helped put into words the feelings generated by the beauty and wonder of the coast of Maine.

Bill Kingston

It's seven-thirty on a balmy, placid August morning. In Perkins Cove in Ogunquit, on Maine's southeast coast, Captain Bill Kingston brings the party-fishing boat *Ugly Anne* alongside a float where an eager group of some thirty "flatlanders" is waiting to board for a morning of deep-sea fishing. Overhead, two herring gulls screech raucously in the tangy, salty air.

At eight sharp, the boat pulls away from the dock, heads out the narrow neck of the harbor's entrance, and into the open ocean, riding gracefully on the gentle, oily swells.

"We're here to go fishing, not catching," Bill announces as the *Ugly Anne* heads eastward toward stark, forbidding Boon Island Light, some six miles offshore, searching for bluefish, striped bass, rock cod, and haddock. Bill tries to make the whole experience an adventure, knowing full well that not everyone will catch something worth bringing home.

As the land recedes, the shape of the coastline becomes apparent. Aside from the monadnock Mount Agamenticus, the land's profile is a flat sliver lying between a cerulean blue sea and an indigo sky.

The coast of Maine officially begins in the middle of the Piscataqua River, across from Portsmouth, New Hampshire. This southern section of the coast swings gently northeastward, marked not by a craggy, granite-walled coast, but rather by relatively low, rocky headlands, tied together by sweeping bands of sand beach.

Along this section of Maine's coast, protected anchorages are scarce. From Kittery, which sits on the Piscataqua, to Portland Head Light, guarding the entrance to Casco Bay, those that exist are found at the mouths of short, natural rivers. Among such harbors are York, Kennebunkport, and Cape Porpoise. One, Bill Kingston's

own Perkins Cove, is manmade, dredged by the Army Corps of Engineers in 1941.

"Perkins is unique," Bill says. "All the moorings here are used by fishermen. It's not really a harbor for transients. The moorings are attached to heavy iron chains that run along the cove's bottom from east to west. The boats are moored from both bow and stern to minimize swing room."

"What do locals think of yachtsmen?" Bill asks rhetorically. "Well, they're tolerated as long as they are competent, gentlemanly, and respectful of the fishermen's trade."

Perkins Cove, with its wooden bascule bridge, is a man-made harbor, dredged in 1941. Space is very tight. All moorings are secured fore and aft to large iron chains that lie across the harbor floor.

Backlit by the October sun, a lobster boat slips into Pepperell Cove at Kittery Point, right on the Maine–New Hampshire border. On the horizon is Whaleback Light, marking the entrance to the Piscataqua River, which divides the two states.

In the spring, Kittery Point harbormaster John McCollett supervises putting in the floats at the town dock. He oversees the harbor's 228 moorings, only 13 of which are for commercial vessels. "People used not to mind when things went bump in the night," he says, "but now they are more particular, and we're really maxed out space-wise. We have two hundred people on the waiting list for moorings."

The Back Channel in Kittery offers boating services on the less-traveled section of the Piscataqua River, where it swings around Seavey Island, site of the Portsmouth Naval Shipyard. In 1623 Kittery was the first town to be established in Maine. It was here in 1777 that the American Navy had its beginnings with the launching of the eighteen-gun sloop *Ranger*.

A lobster boat approaches the fisherman's co-op on the Cape Porpoise town dock. This small but well-protected harbor is home to some fifty-five fishing boats and twenty-five pleasure boats. Located about halfway along the route from Portsmouth to Portland, it is one of the best anchorages between the two cities.

There is a world of difference between the harbors in Kennebunkport (below) and Cape Porpoise. While only six miles separate them, the latter is a real working harbor, while the former draws pleasure boats by the dozens. There are many marinas, as well as fine restaurants and shopping, along the narrow Kennebunk River, which was once home to thirty boatyards.

The wind gusts over thirty knots during an early fall nor'easter. The relatively smooth water in Cape Porpoise's harbor, however, is testimony to the excellent protection provided it by the surrounding islands and ledges.

Arching gracefully toward Spain, an ocean away, Fletcher Neck forms the eastern and southern side of Biddeford Pool, a largely tidal body of water. It provides a small anchorage, while Wood Island to the east offers larger but more open shelter. The Pool and the nature sanctuary at the end of Fletcher Neck are excellent bird-watching areas.

York Harbor is one of the prettiest on Maine's southern coast, as well as being one of the state's oldest settlements, founded in 1624. The entrance is tricky, requiring a 180-degree turn to starboard, but this very dogleg makes the anchorage here the great hurricane hole that it is. York Village has many historical homes, and the nearby sweeping sand beaches draw crowds seeking summertime fun.

Not all of Maine's harbors are wrapped in the arms of the land. Seal Cove, only six miles from downtown Portland, is protected from the bold ocean by Seal Rock and Richmond Island.

Casco Bay Region

Lisa Plummer

At ten sharp on a glorious summer morning at a pier in Portland's Old Port, Captain Lisa Plummer gives one long blast on her vessel's horn and eases the Casco Bay ferry *Maquoit II* away from the terminal and into Portland Harbor's busy shipping channel.

Lisa and her four-man crew have 185 passengers under their care as they head east on the daily three-and-a-quarter-hour "mail run." They will stop at five islands: Little Diamond, Great Diamond, Long, Chebeague, and Cliff. These waters know well the hulls of the vessels owned by Casco Bay Lines, for this is the oldest continuously operating ferry company in the United States.

The bay has been the focus of human activity for thousands of years. The Abenaki Indians fished its waters long before what most believe was a visit by the Vikings some one thousand years ago. The name Casco Bay comes from the Spanish *Bahia de Casco*, the moniker used by the sixteenth-century explorer Esteban Gomez. It means "Bay of the Skull (or Helmet)."

"Casco Bay is certainly the most heavily trafficed of Maine's waters," Lisa says as she threads the *Maquoit II* among mammoth oil tankers, colorful kayaks, tacking sailboats, and a seemingly endless slalom course of lobster buoys. "You have to be alert every second. I never know where the next challenge will come from. But, there are quiet moments, too, when I can take in the real beauty of the bay."

It is Casco Bay's islands, as well as its manageable size (some twenty miles wide, with the broadest reach of water measuring only a mile across) that give this body of water its charm. While the area around Portland is busy, a short sail to the north and east opens up an ever-changing display of natural beauty. And the names of the islands one glides by are as delightful as the kaleidoscoping vistas of land and sea: Lower Goose and the Goslings, Charity Ledge, Sow and Pigs, Pumpkin Nob, Pound of Tea, Ministerial, and Junk of Pork. Comprising the Maine coast from Portland Head Light to the west side of Small Point in Phippsburg, just west of the mouth of the Kennebec River, the bay is home to some one hundred and thirty-six such islands, of which only six have year-round inhabitants.

At her first stop, Little Diamond, Lisa supervises the off-loading of building and garden supplies, a sofa, and assorted boxes as passengers disembark. "Running the ferry in the winter is certainly different," she muses as she soaks up the sun's warmth on deck. "Then we have to contend with freezing spray, stronger winds, heavier seas, and visibility problems from snow squalls and sea smoke. But I do love the challenge."

"I really feel that I have the best of both worlds," Lisa continues, "because I can live in one of New England's most cosmopolitan cities while enjoying the natural beauty of Casco Bay. I don't know of any other place on the Maine coast that offers such variety."

A Casco Bay Lines ferry heads for Diamond Cove (right center), the harbor on Great Diamond Island. Across the western arm of Casco Bay stands Portland, Maine's largest city and New England's largest port. It is also the region's busiest, annually shipping $1.8 billion of Maine products and hosting some two hundred and fifteen thousand cruise-ship passengers.

Portland's poet, Henry Wadsworth Longfellow, christened the place of his birth "the beautiful town that is seated by the sea." (His family home is several blocks north of the waterfront.) Greater Portland, which includes a circlet of adjoining towns—some seen in this aerial view—is home to maritime and commercial interests, as well as being a burgeoning service and financial center.

A tanker unloads crude oil, destined for refineries in Canada, at a South Portland dock. Across the harbor, flags snap in the fresh breeze atop the Portland Observatory, indicating that is open to visitors. This 1807 signal station, recently restored to its former glory, offers stunning views of Casco Bay and the entrance to Portland's bustling waterway.

One of the more than forty-five cruise ships that call yearly at Portland Harbor lies alongside the International Ferry Terminal on a sultry summer afternoon. Each vessel's hundreds of passengers typically enjoy the city's historic sites, its cultural opportunities, and its varied boutiques and restaurants.

Sailing is pursued with passion in the Portland area. Day sailors, cruising yachtsmen, and racing enthusiasts not only coexist but are sometimes the same people. The beautiful waters of Casco Bay are easily accessible from many local marinas and yacht clubs, and commutes are short. Many weekend races—like this one, a charity fund-raiser—are easily viewed from the Spring Point Light breakwater in South Portland.

Even some safe harbors can seem scary. Dock personnel of the Portland Yacht Club work purposefully at securing mooring lines and loose halyards as a summer storm kicks up a nasty chop in the anchorage. P.Y.C., located in Falmouth Foreside, is the nation's second oldest yacht club.

Because Jewell Island, on the outer edge of Casco Bay, is such an easy stopover for cruising sailors heading down east, it is usually packed with boats. This single sailboat takes advantage of unusual solitude on a perfect July day.

Lying offshore from the entrance to the Kennebec River, Seguin Island looms high and windswept. For sailors, this is only a good stopover spot, rather than a safe harbor, but the view from the top of the island commands broad expanses east and west in Casco Bay. Under the watchful eye of Seguin Light a pulling boat that is part of the Outward Bound education program shares the anchorage with a lobster yacht.

A foam-flecked sea and roiling clouds mark the passing of a violent storm at the tip of Bailey Island. After one look at the jagged, rocky shore along Jaquish Gut, any mariner will appreciate the fact that a safe harbor, Mackerel Cove, is right around the corner.

White birches stand as stalwart winter sentinels on the shore of Mackerel Cove. By spring, this quiet scene will be charged with the activities of both commercial and pleasure craft. This convenient anchorage lies close to the "express route" running down east, but it serves as a pleasant weekend rendezvous spot, as well.

Cumberland Foreside, a Greater Portland community, provides residents and visiting sailors with morning serenity, as well as convenient access to Maine's biggest metropolis. Sturdivant Island (center), one of the hundreds of islands in Casco Bay, is home to summer residents only.

Midcoast Region
Peter Kass

(Right) Christened by her owner's relatives, a new lobster boat is ready to launch at Johns Bay Boat Yard. (Far right) Peter Kass is one of the few builders still turning out fishing boats in wood.

Tucked into a small inlet near the boat-building and fishing village of South Bristol, just upstream from the mouth of Johns Bay is Peter Kass's Johns Bay Boat Yard. It's a very simple, two-story, shingled structure, worn and grayed by the passage of years. But there is nothing decrepit or weathered about what is produced under its aging roof. For it is here that, one by one, Peter builds his top-of-the-line lobster boats.

This section of Maine, often called the Midcoast, runs approximately from Small Point and the eastern edge of Casco Bay, to Owls Head and the Muscle Ridge Channel, where Penobscot Bay begins. Here the coastline holds some notable harbors and anchorages, among them Boothbay Harbor, Christmas Cove, Friendship, and Tenants Harbor. Offshore are the islands of Monhegan, Seguin, and Damariscove.

"Our part of the coast is pretty chopped up and irregular," says Peter. "We don't have the big, smooth granite of Penobscot Bay or the Casco Bay ledges that run into the bay like wood grain." Instead, he explains, this stretch gets its character from the many rivers that reach the sea here, carving the shoreline into thin, rocky peninsulas separated by deep estuaries and bays. The area is home both to great rivers such as the Kennebec and Sheepscot, and to small ones such as the Damariscotta, Johns, Medomak, and St. George.

This type of coastline allows for maximum access to the water, making it a great location for a boatbuilder, with many suppliers nearby. "I like working with wood," Peter says, "and I buy that and my other materials from small, local contractors. For instance, when I need cedar for planking, I go to a lumberman I know. We go out to the woods together to select the trees that are then milled exactly to my specs."

These specs are very precise. The fishermen love Peter's work. He has a list of waiting customers, but in twenty-one years of building boats, he has never advertised. Satisfied owners and word-of-mouth have been all the promotion he has needed.

Does Peter ever have a chance to spend time on the water? "Oh, yes," he replies, "I take some long weekends and get away. My favorite anchorage is Criehaven, on Ragged Island—it's so remote, peaceful, and pretty. That's a beautiful island to walk around, right on the edge of the wide-open sea. It's a wonderful place on a summer night."

The Gut in South Bristol, near Peter Kass's boat-yard, is a working harbor where many fishermen repair their traps during the winter, when the lobsters have moved offshore.

The quietude of a late afternoon in summer
sweeps softly across the still harbor of Christmas
Cove at the end of the South Bristol peninsula.
This cove was first recorded in nautical litera-
ture by Captain John Smith, who spent Decem-
ber 25th here in 1614. Though by no means
undiscovered, the harbor has a quiet dignity that
residents and visitors alike seem to honor.

Not all harbors are close to the open ocean. Damariscotta, about fourteen miles from the sea, sits at the head of the Damariscotta River, one of the many tidal waterways that typify the mid-coast region. Some eleven thousand years ago, the glaciers that once covered Maine with mile-thick ice retreated. The valleys they had scoured between ridges of granite were slowly filled by the sea, leaving a coastline marked by long rocky fingers that seem to clutch at the ocean.

The Antique Boat Parade, one of the many events centered around Windjammer Days at the end of June, has been a Boothbay tradition for over forty years. The broad harbor is surrounded by an eclectic mix of touristy shops, restaurants, and galleries. These rub shoulders with lobster co-ops, marine services, and bait shacks, making Boothbay Harbor a boat watcher's paradise.

Linekin Bay, separated from Boothbay Harbor only by Spruce Point, is a broad, well-protected bay, as quiet and unspoiled as Boothbay is bustling and developed. Linekin is a favorite anchorage of many passenger-schooner captains, especially during Windjammer Days.

An aerial view of Cozy Harbor and the adjacent
Sheepscot River shows why the anchorage is so
well-protected. While the grip of winter limits activity here, in the summer the harbor and river
are alive with fleets of small sailboats from the
harbor's Southport Yacht Club, darting hither
and yon like small clouds of graceful butterflies.

Snuggled into the western shore of Southport Island, on the Sheepscot River, is Cozy Harbor (spelled "Cosy" by the locals, in the original Old English). Cozy it is. Shaped like an appendix, this anchorage is beautifully protected from the weather, but space is tight, indeed. Its narrow entrance and small size limits its capacity to vessels not much larger than lobster boats. To the left of the yacht club pier is the Earl W. Pratt General Merchandising Store. Founded in 1919, it is still run today by Earl's son, Gus, who took over from his dad in 1937.

Built in 1857, Marshall Point Light marks the primary entrance to Port Clyde, which was an important shipbuilding community in the nineteenth century but is now economically dependent on commercial fishing. From here, it is an hour's passenger ferry ride to Monhegan, one of the most beautiful islands off the Maine coast.

The forty-eight-foot-high Cuckolds Light is anchored on a barren ledge at the southern tip of Southport Island, enticing boats to Boothbay Harbor, some five miles from the open sea. Maine's sixty-seven lighthouses are the source of many tales, both tall and true. Although all the towers are now automated, the sight of a stalwart light silhouetted against the angry sky of a growing storm can bring to mind stirring images of a lone lighthouse keeper battling the elements to save the lives of mariners.

As one cruising guide puts it, "New Harbor is anything but." It has been a fishing center for nearly four hundred years. The first properly executed land deed in New England was signed on this spot in 1625 by John Brown and Chief Samoset. Although a possible refuge from a sudden storm, this harbor is crammed with draggers and lobster boats. Visiting yachtsmen are better served by heading north a bit to other harbors along the western shore of Muscongus Bay.

Fresh seafood always seems to taste best when eaten by the edge of the sea. Beside Five Islands Harbor, which really *is* comprised of five islands, a family waits to enjoy a typical Maine lobster dinner, complete with corn-on-the-cob, coleslaw, baked potato, and blueberry pie.

A full summer moon rises over the Sheepscot River, flooding the harbor at Five Islands in a gentle glow. By boat, the trip across the river to Cozy Harbor is only a mile, but by car the same excursion would require a drive of some forty miles, up one long rocky peninsula and then down another.

The westward view from Monhegan Island's Lighthouse Hill sweeps across Monhegan Village, Manana Island, and Muscongus Bay. Located ten miles offshore, Monhegan's cliffs tower 160 feet above the Atlantic. The island is called by some "Maine's Brigadoon" because of its isolated, otherworldly qualities. Its remoteness from the stresses of mainland life seems to magnify Monhegan's natural gift of tranquility. The permanent population of seventy-five swells by over three hundred in the summer.

Damariscove Island, four miles offshore from the entrance to Boothbay Harbor, is now owned by the Nature Conservancy and has no year-round residents (other than rats!). The situation was quite different four hundred years ago, when this was a year-round fishing and trading station. The harbor is narrow but well-protected. A former Coast Guard station, now privately owned, is one of a very few signs of human habitation since the last island dwellers left in the 1930s.

A lobster boat heads to sea past some small islands in the Hockomock Channel, at the head of Muscongus Bay, just west of Friendship. The Maine coast is blessed with over thirty-five hundred islands, more than in the entire Caribbean. About half of them are publicly owned; only a dozen or so are occupied all year.

Penobscot Bay Region
Neal Parker

*Neal Parker, captain
of the schooner-
yacht* Wendameen.

Captain Neal Parker, owner, restorer, and master of the sixty-seven-foot 1912 schooner *Wendameen*, knows Penobscot Bay very well indeed. When he's not at the helm taking up to fourteen guests on overnight cruises from her homeport of Rockland, he's dreaming about voyages to come.

With unbridled enthusiasm Neal says, "One only has to look at a chart to see that Penobscot Bay is a wide-open playground. It's comprised of two large, open bodies of water—the east and the west bays—both incredibly well-protected from the Atlantic Ocean. If you try to do any cruising down in southern Maine, you find you have the choice of either staying in tiny little inlets or narrow passageways that run north and south. Or, you go offshore on days when you might otherwise consider not heading offshore.

"On the other hand, no matter how hard the wind is blowing in Penobscot Bay, it seems you can always have a nice day of sailing out here. We're protected from the elements—the harshest elements—on all sides. Only on an unusual day does it get uncomfortable out on the bay."

Neal warns, however, "You always have to expect the unexpected. I remember one night we anchored in Owls Head, and the wind was supposed to come up southeasterly from twenty to thirty knots. I thought, Okay, we're snug as a bug in a rug here. We had a charming time till after dinner, when the wind hauled around to the northeast and then just blew like stink. It must have been forty knots in there, and our bowsprit was going underwater with every other wave. We had our second anchor down, and it was a sleepless night for everyone."

One of the questions most asked by Captain Parker's passengers is, "How deep is the water?"

"What I do is point out the Camden Hills and tell them that what's underneath us is tenfold more dramatic," explains Neal. "The depth in Penobscot Bay is constantly changing. The same geological phenomena that created those hills also contributed to the contour of the bottom. You can be sailing along in two hundred feet of water, but within a couple of a hundred yards, a rock breaks the surface."

The captain of the *Wendameen* goes on to say, "I think that contributed to keeping yachtsmen away for many years: People didn't know how to read charts, didn't know how to do basic navigation. They were extremely cautious about coming up to this part of the coast of Maine. You combine those bottom contours with a little bit of fog, and it's easy enough to get into trouble out here."

But with global-positioning systems (GPS) and plenty of electronic navigational aids, Penobscot Bay has become one of the most popular cruising grounds in the Northeast. And, Neal adds, that's for a very good reason: "If you took the entire state of Maine, condensed it, and put it in a can, you'd get Penobscot Bay. We have mountains, we have shore, we have islands, we have cities, we have towns. We have everything right here."

And there are the windjammers. From May to October, it's rare to look seaward from Camden or Castine or Vinalhaven or Rockland and not see at least one of these graceful vessels. Under billowing sails with their flags snapping in the wind, they slice through the blue waters of Penobscot Bay. They are powerful visual reminders of a time now past, a time very close to Neal Parker's heart.

Gliding into the arch of a welcoming rainbow, the *Wendameen* enters Pulpit Harbor on the island of North Haven, one of the storied shelters in central Penobscot Bay.

Perched like a wise old bird on the western branch of Penobscot Bay, at the entrance to Rockland Harbor, is Owls Head and its prominent lighthouse. Owls Head Light, now automated, is accessible by land and offers stunning views of the bay and Muscle Ridge Channel.

Strong tidal currents run along the scoured granite shores of High Island in the Muscle Ridge Channel. Stone quarried on these islands during the late 1800s graces city buildings in cities such as New York, Washington, and Charleston.

Most lobstermen take their colorful and individualized buoys and traps ashore during the season of cold and ice, when lobsters crawl far offshore, into deep water. This gear is in Owls Head Harbor, a snug fisherman's anchorage. Nearby is the notable Owls Head Transportation Museum, a fascinating assemblage of antique airplanes and vehicles.

A fleet of restored wooden schooners, locally called windjammers, hails from the ports of Rockland, Rockport, and Camden. These vessels offer vacations for folks eager to sample life aboard a wind-powered boat, where they enjoy bounteous meals, gorgeous sunsets, and the opportunity to become "adopted" crewmen. This schooner's bowsprit looms above a bevy of dinghies that serve as mini-ferries between cruising boats and the delights of shore.

The thin, gray line of the breakwater that forms Rockland's harbor ends with the exclamation point of a lighthouse. Measuring 4,346 feet long and constructed of giant blocks of Vinalhaven granite, the breakwater was built by the Army Corps of Engineers beginning in 1881.

Maine's native Americans called Rockland "the great landing place." Today the waterfront hosts a congenial mix of fishermen, ferry passengers, and "from-away" visitors to Maine. Even on less fair days, when fog and salt scent the air and seagulls come ashore to perch on the harbor's pilings, Rockland provides security and all the necessities and amenities.

Rockport Harbor, tucked between Rockland and Camden, has a maritime past as well as an industrial history, for it was the center of the lime industry in the 1800s. Remains of the kilns still stand on the waterfront, as does a statue of André the harbor seal, Rockport's most illustrious traveler.

Although Rockport is wide open to southern
swells, causing "rolly" nights aboard, it remains
a very popular harbor for tourists and for people
cruising the Maine coast. Summer and year-
round homes surround this picturesque harbor,
whose shape resembles a sea bag.

The Camden Hills and Mount Battie—visible from
all thirty square miles of Penobscot Bay—serve as
a secure and serene backdrop to Camden's famous
safe harbor. A year-round community, the town
offers all facilities, wonderful shopping and dining,
and a culturally cosmopolitan élan.

Camden's inner harbor provides berths for a kaleidoscope of boats, from skiffs and Herreshoff cats to sleek power craft and graceful dowager schooners. In summer, the town is abloom with an array of visitors who appreciate its waterfront charm and capacity. But during the off-season, which in Maine is more than six months long, even cabin-fever sufferers can find cheery respite from winter's woes here.

Many schooners that call Penobscot Bay harbors their home ports have no engines, as they were originally built for wind power alone. Consequently, each of these vessels requires maneuvering assistance from a mighty midget—its yawl boat—an example of which is just visible under the transom of the windjammer *Mercantile*.

Dignified matrons totally at home in their environment, two windjammers sweep along West Penobscot Bay off Rockport, catching the prevailing southwesterly breeze. This view from Beech Hill takes in the northern end of North Haven Island and, beyond, some of Deer Isle.

Lobster, corn, clams, potatoes, and sometimes
other goodies—all steamed in a seaweed "oven"—
create the classic lobster bake. This one is being
served on the gravel beach of Warren Island, at
the northern entrance to Islesboro's Gilkey
Harbor. Windjammer passengers chilled by the
damp sea air are soon warmed from within by
the sumptuous, hearty fare and the camaraderie.

Three miles off Penobscot Bay's western shore,
Islesboro offers a golden summer existence for its
devotees, as is evidenced by a sunset viewed from
the deck of a windjammer. Seven Hundred Acre
Island, adjacent to the ten-mile expanse of Islesboro, forms broad Gilkey Harbor with its several
anchorages. Year-round citizens are served by a
ferry that runs between nearby Grindel Point and
Lincolnville, on the mainland.

Named for its ecclesiastical resemblance, Pulpit Rock guards the entrance to Pulpit Harbor on North Haven. For over a century, osprey families have delivered their shrill sermons from the huge nest of sticks and sea grasses that tops the pinnacle.

As the sun drops lower in the west, a sloop heads for safe harbor and the satisfying completion of a day of sailing among Penobscot Bay's many spruce-topped granite islands. The homey pleasures of food and drink on deck, absorbing nature's beauty at anchor, bring to mind the expression "Maine—the way life should be."

Hard as it may be to think about hurricanes on an
evening of such placid, luminous calm, Pulpit Harbor has the highest rating among safe harbors as a
"hurricane hole." It has long been popular among
windjammers as a Friday-night haven prior to their
crossing the bay on Saturday to pick up new passengers. In such benign conditions, the gaff-rigged
mainsail is often left up until nightfall.

A summer vacation cruise could conceivably encompass only Vinalhaven, with its collection of protected and scenic anchorages. Named for early settlers whose descendants still fish these waters, Vinalhaven is the larger of the two Fox Islands, the other being North Haven.

Fiercely independent, able, and resourceful, Maine lobstermen such as these at Carvers Harbor are a veritable legend. Braving fog and high winds, rising early and doing backbreaking work, they ply their inherited profession because of a deep commitment to the sea.

Wooden lobster "cars" float in a quiet cove in Carvers Harbor, at the southern end of Vinalhaven. Within each one, lobsters remain alive in their natural saltwater environment until circumstances such as price dictate that the catch be sent to market. Currently, a yearly average of over 54 million pounds of Maine lobsters are sent worldwide to provide a treat for diners.

Perry Creek, on Vinalhaven, is actually closer to North Haven's town than to the one at Carvers Harbor. It is another "safest" harbor, being slim and snug and totally protected from gales. Its popularity is evident even on a benign summer's eve.

A catboat awaits the lifting of morning fog before departing spruce-surrounded peace. The "wishbone" allows the mainsail (shown furled on the boom) to be raised and lowered safely and easily by a solo sailor. The comfortable beam, or width, of this vessel makes for generous accommodations below, in the cabin.

White sails and white fair-weather clouds appropriately adorn the White Islands on a perfect July day. Sprinkled a bit sou'west of Vinalhaven, this mini-archipelago exhibits the type of granite that was quarried here and shipped far and wide.

Seen from a point near the footbridge at the head of the harbor, Belfast and its snug anchorage offer something for commercial- and pleasure-boat owners alike. This former shipbuilding center is blessed with wonderful examples of Federal and Victorian architecture. And each summer, "BearFest" presents over fifty life-size bears artistically representing both whimsy and reality.

A variety of boats lie at the Belfast City Landing as their variety of owners follow simple summer pursuits. Some go crabbing, some picnic, some sunbathe. Others load, hose down, stock up, empty, and maneuver. There's nothing remarkable, but everything is satisfying on a crystal summer Saturday.

Business and pleasure coexist in Bucksport, at the head of Penobscot Bay. As the summer sea breeze picks up, lots of people in lots of small watercraft get out on the Penobscot River in the shadow of the looming International Paper mill.

Rowboats and dinghies are left high and dry at low tide in Eggemoggin Reach's Naskeag Harbor. For the cruising sailor, some obstructions—such as these boulders—are clearly evident, while others—such as sandbars—are more elusive. Many of Maine's harbors offer this kind of solitude and serenity.

Spectators and crews enjoy the finish of the Eggemoggin Reach Regatta at the WoodenBoat School's "campus" in Brooklin. Here the craft of building boats in wood is nurtured and shared in the lee of the Babson Islands.

Eggemoggin Reach enfolds many a favorite anchorage, including Center Harbor. The owner and operator of the highly respected boatyard here is Steve White, grandson of East Blue Hill resident E. B. White (now deceased), who wrote the children's classic *Charlotte's Web*, among other best-selling books.

The safest harbors are safe *always*, no matter how hard or from where the wind blows. Often, however, sailors can opt for an anchorage best suited for specific conditions. For example, Weir Cove, on Cape Rosier, offers particularly good protection from strong northerlies. The tiny purplish sea heather flowers in the foreground appear in early August along the tidal zone.

"It's gonna blow . . . with the next shift of the tide . . ." are familiar words to generations of parents and children who know Buck Harbor, in South Brooksville, from author Robert McCloskey's classic *Time of Wonder*. Today the weather is just foggy and drizzly—time for clam chowder and a cozy game of Parcheesi below while waiting for a better sailing day. Buck Harbor is also a "safest" hurricane hole.

Maine Maritime Academy's training ship, the *State of Maine*, is moored in Castine. Here she is seen from Lords Cove in West Brooksville, on the Bagaduce River. Sea kayaking has become a popular outdoor experience along the Maine coast, offering a different vantage point for viewing harbors and marine life.

The wide vista from the entrance to Castine Harbor opens to the Camden Hills and looks much as it did centuries ago. The town's prominent location near the head of Penobscot Bay made it a desirable and exchangeable pawn among European powers. In 1614 Castine was held by the French. For the next two hundred years it repeatedly changed hands, first going to the British, then the Dutch, then the Americans, the British, the Americans, and the British. Finally, the Americans gained permanent possession at the end of the War of 1812.

The passenger schooner *Grace Bailey* slips gracefully by the Castine waterfront as she heads out to share summer pleasures with a less regimented crew than the academy cadets aboard the *State of Maine*, which dwarfs her.

Pumpkin Island Light, just north of Little Deer Isle, marks the western end of Eggemoggin Reach. Soft layers of haze and mist define the profile of distant hills in Lincolnville and Searsmont.

Mount Desert Region

Ted Hoskins

For many years, Reverend Ted Hoskins was the minister on the Maine Seacoast Mission Society's vessel Sunbeam, *based in Northeast Harbor.*

Envision a minister whose firsthand knowledge of the waters around Mount Desert and the adjacent islands is as great as his knowledge of the Bible. That would be the Reverend Ted Hoskins.

Ted first came to Maine in 1941, the son of the summer minister on Isle Au Haut. He has had an abiding love and respect for the area and its people ever since. Recently he served for eight years as minister on the Maine Seacoast Mission Society's seventy-two-foot steel vessel *Sunbeam*. This vessel and the nondenominational staff it carries bring pastoral work, mediation and crisis-intervention services, food aid and medical care, as well as other assistance to those who live on Maine's outer islands.

All this time at sea in the Mount Desert area has given Ted a real sense of the region. "Its physical characteristics are quite different from the rest of coastal Maine," he says. "The mountains are bald pieces of granite that stick up into the sky like nowhere else along the coast. Of course, there are winds that work them, because they're great slides for the breeze. They come off—*woooosh*—right down to the shore. Sailors love that extra strength of wind off these mountains!"

And speaking of weather on the coast of Maine, Ted says, "If you don't have specific plans, it's always perfect because it gives you the excuse to either go ahead and do what you wanted to do or not do it or wish you'd done it yesterday or postpone it until tomorrow. It's so marvelously,

magnificently unpredictable! One of the sad things is all these forecasts that you get. Now, they're important if you're fish'n. If you know the wind's goin' to come up hard in the afternoon, well, that's good 'cause you won't set out to do somethin' and just have to turn around and come back. But there's somethin' nice about meeting the day and discovering what it holds. There's a good feeling about not having it all figured out."

He goes on to explain, "In lots of areas you get a little breeze com'n or you're in a fog, and you can just watch the water a little bit and pretty well tell where you're goin'. You can't do that around Mount Desert. You learn very quickly to be mindful of all the signs as to which way the water's flowin' and where the wind's comin' from because that just changes. If you don't have a compass eye, you'll be in trouble."

Ted Hoskins has a lot of admiration and regard for the men and women who wrest a living from the frigid Gulf of Maine waters in the Mount

Desert area. "The local people who get jobs on board yachts and vessels of all kinds or go to the Maine Maritime Academy—they're among the best, mainly because they've grown up with having to keep their senses alive, really reading the water and the wind, and paying attention."

Aboard the *Sunbeam*, Ted's busy time was in the winter, when he'd try to schedule two visits per island per month. "Probably the most important thing I did in my job as minister was just to be present where the people lived and worked, to be available in whatever way was needed. Everybody knew I was a pastor, that I had services. Everybody knew that this had nothing to do with whether or not I knew them."

Ted reflects for a moment on what spirituality means to many islanders. "The religion is not so much sittin' in church pews and sing'n songs and hear'n a sermon as it is the overall sense that there's a caring in the world for this creation—and we were on the islands to represent that."

On a late winter afternoon, the low sun highlights the complexities of the coastline of Mount Desert: the Cranberry Isles in the foreground, the Bass Harbor Head peninsula above them, and some of the myriad Penobscot Bay islands beyond. This panorama dramatically illustrates the beauties and difficulties of sailing one of the world's most challenging and satisfying cruising grounds.

Barnacle tough while at the same time seductively beautiful, the town of Stonington rises like an amphitheater up the south-facing shore of its ample harbor.

A full September moon softens Stonington's mus-
cular harbor, bringing a dreamy quiet to this
normally bustling center of fishing activity. Of
the approximately fifteen hundred residents,
fully one-third have commercial licenses.

As a storm rolls in, Stonington's fishing fleet lies snug in its harbor. In summer, the weather tends to come from the southwest, but in winter, it moves in from the northwest. Occasionally, however, the winter wind will shift to the northeast, bringing with it arctic cold and driving wind or snow.

Granite is physically and literally Stonington's foundation, as it was stone quarries that gave the town both its name and its economic reason for being. From the 1870s to the 1920s, this industry was the key to the town's prosperity. Stonington granite was used for office buildings, bridges, monuments, and museums up and down the East Coast. But with the advent of elevators and the use of steel in skyscrapers, the need for granite all but disappeared.

Raising sheep on the coast of Maine has been a tradition for hundreds of years. The climate is ideal and, especially on the islands, there is a lack of predators. Burnt Cove, the harbor here, is just around the corner from Stonington and a stone's throw from Crotch Island, where the quarrying industry is undergoing a mini-revival.

The distinctive silhouette of Robinson Point Light marks the entrance to the Isle au Haut (pronounced "aisle-ah-hoe") Thorofare. This long, narrow harbor serves the seventy "year-'rounders," who like to live close to their fishing grounds.

Isle au Haut, measuring 556 feet high, six miles long, and two miles wide, is some eight miles south of Stonington, the Deer Isle Thorofare, and the Merchants Row archipelago. More than half the island is part of Acadia National Park, where access is tightly controlled to maintain its wild and fragile beauty.

The warm, pine-scented air and the soft quiet of an early-summer morning in the Isle au Haut Thorofare will be but a pleasant memory as winter approaches, and the lobstermen head out to haul their traps in the frigid predawn darkness.

Someone once said that Frenchboro is "fifty minutes [from the mainland] and fifty years away." The isolation these communities have to cope with can be very trying. They must continually deal with the restrictions of island life. Tempting though it may be, any television ad for a special at the "nearby" burger chain is an empty promise.

About nine miles south of the tip of Mount Desert lies Long Island and its tenacious community of Frenchboro, nestled into the hillside at the end of Lunt Harbor. It takes special people to put up with this sort of remoteness. Reverend Ted Hoskins says that Frenchboro "is like an extended family, with new people finding a way to be a part of the island community. These newcomers work very hard. And they try—as hard as any islander—to look to the future and ask, 'How can we continue?' "

Ragged Island, also called Criehaven, is Maine's most remote inhabited island. Located some twenty-five miles from the mainland at the very edge of the deep Atlantic, it is one of the destinations of the *Sunbeam*. A member of this fishing community once said, "There's only one island off the coast of Maine—and that's the one I live on. It happens to be the center of the earth. Life generates from this island. It isn't for everyone by any means!"

The town of Blue Hill lies beneath its nine-hundred-foot namesake, which does look blue from distant points throughout Penobscot Bay and the surrounding islands. Who knows? In August, during the peak of the wild-blueberry season, the effect may be even more pronounced.

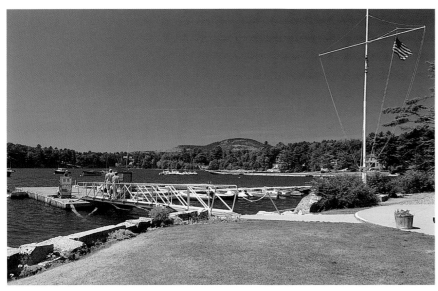

"Blue hill on shining green water" is the definition of the Penobscot tribal word "Kollegewidgwok." The yacht club in Blue Hill Harbor also carries this name. Shining green water extends to the town center only at high tide, but there is plenty of depth elsewhere in this good-sized anchorage, regardless of the time of day.

Maine's significant tides offer both challenges and benefits to boat operators. (It's much better to run aground on a rising than a falling tide!) The tides also provide a dual vision of seascapes such as this one, in East Blue Hill's McHeard Cove. Mudflats, stray kelp, and rockweed-encased ledges punctuate the early dawn.

Cruise ships call frequently at Bar Harbor, tucked into the base of Cadillac Mountain (named for an Indian chief, not an automobile). The town offers a smörgasbord of activities, shops, restaurants, and tours. This is a harbor for those whose preference is not the quiet "gunkhole."

A sturdy, seaworthy lobster boat passes a sleek,
glossy power yacht as the day begins. Farther out
in the harbor floats an Aegis destroyer, built by
Maine's Bath Iron Works. Bar Harbor caters to
each boat owner's needs, as well as to a parade of
visitors eager to experience Maine's beauty.

"Messing about in boats," phraseology from the book *Wind in the Willows*, seems to satisfy many levels of human need. Bar Harbor shelters its fleet behind a long sandbar running from the mainland to Bar Island. This family of spruce-spiked islands is called The Porcupines.

"The Cat," stealthy, swift, and even bewhiskered, is a catamaran ferry that streaks between Bar Harbor and Nova Scotia, Canada, making the crossing in under three hours. The vessel is larger than it looks, carrying 900 passengers and 240 cars and trucks.

The entrance to Northeast Harbor leads to a storied haven. This "Park Avenue" of down-east harbors lies at the southern end of Mount Desert Island. Gracious "cottages," many built at the end of the nineteenth century, surround the snug anchorage. This is also home port to the *Sunbeam*, the nondenominational pastoral ship that ministers to the Maine islands.

One-design sloops return to Northeast Harbor on a spinnaker run, with a spanking southwest breeze directly behind them. With the *monts deserts* (barren mountains) shouldering above the harbor, area yachtsmen are blessed with spectacular views and fair winds.

As one owner of a mooring in Northeast Harbor puts it, "We're really inside here. You don't get any better harbor than this one. You come right around the corner, and you don't get any sea here at all." It is no wonder that Northeast Harbor's town dock attracts watercraft of all sizes and shapes. There are ferries and water taxies and dinghies and sailboats and power boats. Taking a seat in the Sunday sunshine for "boat watching" can bring quiet pleasure for hours.

This southerly view of the entrance to Somes Sound, the only true fjord on Maine's coast, is from the top of Acadia Mountain in the national park of the same name. Reaching the peak involves an hour's hike—not a very strenuous one—and in the right season there are wild blueberries trailside for nibbling.

At the landward end of Somes Sound are some anchorages in addition to Somes Harbor, which is linked to the sound by a narrow gut. It is easy to imagine that life in the slow lane is still cherished here. This harbor offers quiet respite from a long day on the water.

Eagle Cliffs tower over Valley Cove at the ocean end of Somes Sound. This is a historic and favorite anchorage for many cruising sailors. The water is so deep that it is possible to tie a stern line right to the cliffs and jump ashore. A rushing stream, Man-o'-War Brook, can provide a summer shower or a refreshing drink for the boat-bound pet.

The western mountains of Mount Desert's Acadia National Park form the backdrop for the inner section of Bass Harbor. While this anchorage is home to the largest fleet of lobster boats on Mount Desert, it also has facilities and room for many pleasure boats.

As the sun rises over Bass Harbor, a lobsterman leaves a float and heads for his boat. Aside from a large fishing fleet, Bass Harbor is also the point of origin for the ferry service to Frenchboro and Swans Island.

Southwest Harbor is a busy center, with a Coast Guard Station, fishing boats, yachts, marine services, and a year-round town. Its location, within view of many of Acadia's mountains, offers a unique experience. Dawn breaks while the boats in the harbor are still idle; soon the liquid, mercury like sea will be swarming with activity.

Seal Cove, around the corner from Bass Head, is a small gem for those who like getting away from it all. A goodly number of Maine's harbors are either too deep or too rocky for anchoring, but this cove's muddy bottom makes it a good place to drop a hook in all winds but a strong southwesterly.

Bartlett Narrows is a scenic passage leading to other harbors in Blue Hill Bay or to the western shore of Mount Desert Island. In the background is Bartlett Island, the second largest in Blue Hill Bay.

Iced with snow, the many islands of Merchants
Row glitter in hibernation. These small granite-
and-fir nuggets offer a wonderful array of choices
for summer sailing pleasure and safe harbor. Isle
au Haut is the large island in the upper right.

Little Cranberry Island features a dazzling view of the Mount Desert peaks to the northwest. The lobster pound at the end of the gangway holds a fresh catch to be purchased by local folk or passing yachtsmen.

The Hockamock Head light guards the entrance to Burnt Coat Harbor on Swans Island, where a schooner lazes at anchor on a summer morning. No jackets were torched here; the name was originally French—*cote brulé*, or "burnt coast"—because a forest fire had decimated the shore just before it was discovered by Samuel de Champlain in 1604.

Slightly northwest of Swans Island is uninhabited
Buckle Island and its peaceful, well-protected
harbor. This is one of those perfect anchorages for
sitting back and enjoying a passage well-sailed, a
summer sunset, the gentle rocking of the sea, the
hint of sun-warmed spruces in the air. Topped off
by the rich, tangy aroma of freshly harvested
mussels steaming in the galley and the whisper of
an evening breeze stirring the pines ashore, what
could be better?

Down East Region
Colby Young

Colby Young, a third-generation fisherman from Corea, says of the lobster that provides his livelihood, "If God made anything better, He kept it for Himself."

The "Bold Coast," "Down East," "Land of the Pointed Firs"—there are many names for this section of Maine. It's a diamond-hard edge that stands stalwart and strong against the power of the North Atlantic and is the first landfall of the sun each day.

Roughly speaking, down-east Maine begins east of Mount Desert Island and Frenchman's Bay. Compared to the relatively protected waters of Penobscot Bay and the island-sheltered harbors and anchorages of Merchants Row and Mount Desert, the open waters here can bring a rude awakening to the visiting yachtsman. Everything seems to increase in scale after rounding Schoodic Point: The fog gets thicker, the tides stronger (up to twenty vertical feet of change), and the sea less forgiving.

As Colby Young, a third-generation lobsterman fishing out of the classic working harbor of Corea, says about his section of coastline, "The basic geography of the land is not suited for marinas and such like that 'cause we've got too much open ocean. There's no shelters."

But Colby is very much aware of changes coming to the down-east fishermen's way of life. "The full brunt of the tourist population hasn't caught up with us yet. It's comin' fast, but we've still got open space. They haven't come down on us the way they have in the Bar Harbor and Boothbay areas."

Of his fellow lobstermen, Colby says, "Compared to, say, Casco Bay, there's more cama-

raderie among the fishermen. If one gets sick or breaks a leg, the other guys will run his gear for him. They live in each others dooryards. You always see the guys sitt'n around, shoot'n the bull, telling lies and sea stories and stuff like that. We're so far away from everything. You've got to count on each other."

Aside from his lobstering business, Colby is one of the town of Gouldsboro's deputy harbormasters. "We have five or six harbors with working vessels in them. If someone needs a mooring and we have space, we try to get a mooring down for them. The harbormaster has quite a lot of authority if he wants to use it. We're go-betweens. If there are boats that interfere with each other, why, we settle that, get one to move, more or less keep the peace. He adds with a wry smile, "We don't get uptight about something like that the way you would if you were in Bar Harbor or Boothbay Harbor. That's because they have such an influx of pleasure boats. We have a few transients in the summer—a dozen to fifteen sailboats and once in a while, maybe a power boat. If there's a mooring available, we'll put 'em on it."

While river mouths serve as friendly shelters from the Piscataqua at Kittery to the Penobscot at Bucksport, the down-east coast is devoid of major rivers. Instead, places such as Bunkers Harbor, Winter Harbor, and Cutler sit in narrow defiles on the rocky coast.

A striking exception is Roque Island, just

east of Jonesport. At first glance, it looks as if it were transplanted from the Caribbean. New-moon shaped, white-sand beaches form the crossbar of Roque's H-shape. Its beauty, mystery, and remoteness are a powerful magnet drawing sailors to the down-east coast.

Save for Bucks Harbor in Machais Bay, the only noteworthy shelter between Roque Island and Lubec, to the east, is Cutler, a quintessential working harbor tucked deftly in behind Little River Island and its fifty-six-foot lighthouse.

One can tell by the number of skiffs on the moorings in Corea's safe, tight harbor that many fishing boats have left to tend their traps on this foggy summer morning. Lobstering is a rugged, challenging profession—one not for the lazy. Most boats are underway an hour before sunrise, when the air is fresh and heavy with the smell of the sea, and the sound of the gulls rankles the air.

At the head of Frenchman's Bay, enjoying a perfect panorama of the peaks of Mount Desert, is
the town of Sullivan. On a settled summer
evening, this is a wonderful spot to drop the
hook. And, upon awakening, cruising sailors may
have the chance to watch draggers such as these
crisscross the bay, seeking a catch of mussels for
today's burgeoning market.

Though it is far from the fast track to down-east
Maine, many boats "Return to Sorrento" because
of its beauty and pace. Another remarkably picturesque snapshot of Cadillac Mountain and company is readily available in this old summer resort.

Prospect Harbor offers a limited prospect on this
foggy day. Lobster boats are still tied up, awaiting
better weather. These folks are intent on fishing
from the granite outcrops on shore.

Once upon a time, in the 1700s, there was a moose on Becky's Beach. The relevance of this seemingly irrelevant information is the transformation of the name into today's Moosabec Reach! This channel divides Jonesport and Beals Island. Both are serious fishing towns, calling for advanced skills to handle the tricky tides, fog, ledges, and currents in the area.

Not visible from Bucks Harbor on this filmy, soft, gray morning are the nearby Machias Bay aquaculture pens where Atlantic salmon are "farmed." This Maine industry has struggled with hurdles such as fish disease and some environmental opposition, but all sides seem eager to make the important enterprise succeed. Normal, age-old harbor life proceeds at its normal, age-old pace here.

Harborside hay signals the autumnal end of the sailing season. Bucks Harbor, in Machias Bay, is another excellent anchorage nestled in a prosperous fishing town. The seeming remoteness of this spot, way down a peninsula way down east, is belied by the array of U.S. Navy radio communication towers located nearby, on the North Cutler peninsula.

Edged by fish weirs, with Little River Island as a muff-like backdrop, Cutler's intimacy and shelter are immediately apparent. This is a snug, secure, authentic place, and—after sailors beat west from West Quoddy Head, along the steep coastal cliffs where there is no safe refuge—Cutler's charms are all the more welcome.

Eastport is a port of considerable stature, hosting large freighters as well as yachts and fishing boats. Passamaquoddy Bay tides of twenty feet or more are something to be reckoned with and may one day be harnessed as a sorce of electricity. In the foreground, rafts devoted to salmon aquaculture float in Broad Cove, while in the distance the easternmost town in the United States—Lubec—breaks the skyline.

Sea-urchin draggers at the Lubec municipal marina reflect the sunset glow. The town itself seems to be in a moment of economic sunset, despite the beauties and riches of Cobscook and Passamaquoddy Bays. The once-thriving sardine industry has dwindled. Sea urchins, exported to Japan where they are considered a delicacy, are also suffering from overharvesting.

The white-sand crescent in Roque Island Harbor is reminiscent of a Caribbean beach, but the water temperature—even in July—is just fifty degrees! Roque is considered a dream destination for sailors, and it offers a panoply of nifty anchorages. For yachtsmen, this is the last bucolic, unspoiled harbor on the coast of Maine before they sail into Canadian waters.